CCIMBIE6.95

16/8/90

HEINEMANN CHILDREN'S REFERENCE
a division of Heinemann Educational Books Ltd
Halley Court, Jordan Hill, Oxford OX2 8EJ

OXFORD LONDON EDINBURGH
MELBOURNE SYDNEY AUCKLAND
MADRID ATHENS BOLOGNA
SINGAPORE IBADAN NAIROBI HARARE
GABORONE KINGSTON PORTSMOUTH NH(USA)

ISBN 0 431 00324 6

British Library Cataloguing in Publication Data
Bailey, Donna
    We live in the Philippines.
    1.   Philippines. Social life
    I.   Title   II. Sproule, Anna   III. Series
    959.9'046

© Heinemann Educational Books Ltd 1990
First published 1990

Editorial consultant: Donna Bailey
Designed by Richard Garratt Design
Picture research by Jennifer Garratt

Photographs:
Cover: The Hutchison Library (Michael MacIntire)
Colorific Photo Library: 6 (D & J Heaton), 9, 10, 11, 25, 27
    (Marcus Brooke), 13 (Christopher Bain)
Douglas Dickens FRPS: title page, 12, 15, 18, 19, 24, 26, 30, 32
The Hutchison Library: 2, 8, 22, 28, 29, 31 (Michael
    MacIntire), 3, 5, 7, 14, 21 (Dr Nigel Smith), 16, 17, 20, 23
    (C Maurice Harvey)
Robert Harding Picture Library: 4

Printed in Hong Kong

90 91 92 93 94 95 10 9 8 7 6 5 4 3 2 1

We Live in the Philippines

Donna Bailey and Anna Sproule

HEINEMANN

Hello! My name is Meliza.
These are my friends Maria,
Anita, José and Ramon.
We live in the Philippines.

We live in the mountains at Banaue, near
the town of Bontoc, on the island of Luzon.
There are about 7000 islands in the Philippines.
Luzon is one of the biggest islands.

It is very hot in the Philippines so
our house has bamboo walls which
let the air in and keep the house cool.

Dad is a rice farmer and our village
is surrounded by rice fields.
The fields are made from terraces
carved out of the hillside.
The terraces were made over 2000 years
ago by the Ifugao people.

We plant the rice in the terraces
in December when the heavy rains of
the monsoon season are over.
Everybody in the village helps
to plant out the seedlings.

When the rice has been planted we have
a special festival in the village.
Everybody wears the traditional costumes
of the Ifugao people.

The older men wear shell necklaces
and carry spears for the festival.

The women wear brightly coloured skirts
which they weave in the village.
It often rains at this time of the year,
so everyone carries an umbrella.

Ifugao women are famous for their weaving.
They make many different patterns
in the cloth.

During the festival the drummers beat out
the rhythms and we do special dances.
We hope that the rice will grow well and
that we will have a good harvest.

Rice needs a lot of water to grow, so
we flood the hillside terraces with water.
The water is pumped up from the river below.

12

When the rice is ready the fields
are drained and the rice is harvested.
The rice is cut by hand using special knives,
then it is tied in bundles and left
to dry in the sun.

Later the bundles are gathered up and taken to be threshed.
Threshing separates the kernels of rice from the straw.
The children search the fields to find any stalks that have been dropped.

After threshing, there is always
lots of straw left in piles around
the village.

People use this straw to thatch
the roofs of their houses.
Then the rain won't come in during
the monsoon season.

16

During the monsoon season, from June to
October, it rains very hard.
Tourists come to Bontoc and Banaue in
the dry season, from March to May.
They come to see the rice terraces and
to buy the things we make in the village.

In the Philippines tourists travel by bus,
or by special cars called jeepneys.
Jeepneys are like small buses and
carry passengers.
They are usually decorated in bright colours.

18

The tourists come to the mountains
to watch the women in Bontoc
weaving patterns in their cloth.
This woman has even made patterns
on her arms!

The weavers make skirts, bags and clothes
which they sell to the tourists from
stalls by the side of the road.

The tourists also buy shell necklaces
like those worn by the older men
in the village.

One year in May I went by jeepney from
my village to visit my aunt in Manila,
the capital of the Philippines.
On the way there we were held up by
a farmer crossing the road with his ducks.

The farmers on the lowland plain near Manila
grow rice just like we do in the mountains.
This farmer has a water buffalo
to help him plough his fields.

The buffalo also pulls a special sledge
called a pahagad.
The farmer piles the sledge with goods
and rides the buffalo back to his home.

On the plains, people grow lots of
coconuts as well as rice.

The farmers plant the coconut seedlings in
the warm, wet soil where they grow well.
The seedlings soon make coconut palms.

The farmers sell their coconuts, pineapples,
bananas and other fruit from stalls
by the side of the road.

When I arrived in Manila, I was in time
to join in the festival held at the end
of May called Flores de Mayo.
I watched the bands practising
their music before the festival.

The festival is in honour of the Virgin Mary.
Young girls decorate the statue of
the Virgin Mary with flowers.
Then the men carry the statue of the Virgin
from the church.

People from different churches join in
the procession with their statues.
Some carry statues of saints,
others carry statues of bishops.

In the evening there is another procession
by candlelight.
Many of the women wear white veils.
The statues of the Virgin often have blue cloaks.
Blue and white are the Virgin's colours.

The Festival of Santacruzan is also held in May.
The girls dress up in their best clothes and
parade under arches of flowers.
One of the girls is chosen to be
Queen of the Festival.

Index